My Perfect Journal

BY ME & HER

Dedication

To C & H, ALWAYS my rays of sunshine through the clouds –
Thank you x

My Perfect Journal
By A J Gill

ISBN-13: 978-1-5272-0979-4

If you want to be _trusted, be honest, if you want to be honest, be true. Honest, If you want to be true. If you want to be yourself.

THIS JOURNAL BELONGS TO

Charlie
Pullin

THIS IS
ME

PERFECT!

This journal has been inspired by my own life and the experiences I have had along the way. Life can seem much easier to some whilst others let negatives in their own lives overpower the positives leading to a steady downward spiral. This can affect our relationships, friends and nearest and dearest. I would generally classify myself as an optimist with a very positive outlook on life, but still have had times wishing time away so I can get to the weekend, go on holiday or attend a special occasion. I have even counted sleeps and completed a 'chuff chart' (a counting down chart). Looking back, I feel I lost the time I've counted out of my life and I will never get that time back again.

Had a bad day? A bad week? A bad month? Does it seem to go on and on in a downward spiral? This journal is about logging even the tiniest of perfects in your day-to-day life so you can realise that the bad day, week or month isn't all bad. It is about stopping for a few seconds and just taking stock of yourself and identifying just one little bit of positive to help you to realise that it's really all okay and things will improve.

Example: I've had a bad day. I go to bed feeling bad, I wake up feeling bad. The day is bad and then it spirals into a bad week... it is difficult to get out of this, so let's start by taking the first bad day and find a glimmer of positive and log it. It can be anything: a smile, the sound of someone laughing, birds singing, a funny comment, an uplifting, feel-good song, a nice cuppa tea...ANYTHING! Log it, and at the end of your week, you can look back at all the lovely little positives in your world and realise it wasn't all bad after all. Once you begin to recognise the little perfects in every day, it will become a habit. You will begin to find more positives to help you realise the bad days won't last forever.

This journal has been divided into 13 sections of
4 weeks for ease, ideally it should be completed daily
but fill it in as you wish! At the end of each 4 week
block is a page for your random acts of kindness and
a page to put any scripts, photos, tickets from that
period - at the end of the year you will have a year's
worth of 'perfects'.

NB - Colouring is a great way to wind down, relax
and chill out. This journal is full of 'colour me in' pages'
pick which pages and what you want to colour in as you
go, the choice is yours!

BE
CRAZY
BE
WEIRD
BE
YOURSELF

Just a bit about you

ARE YOU A GLASS HALF FULL/HALF EMPTY SORT OF PERSON?

WHY? WHAT MAKES YOU LIKE THAT?

ARE YOU HAPPY?

WOULD YOU LIKE TO BE FRIENDS WITH YOU?

ARE YOU A GOOD FRIEND?

WHAT ARE YOUR BEST QUALITIES?

WHAT IS YOUR PERSONALITY LIKE?

FUNNY BITS/TRIVIA ABOUT YOU:

NOW START LOGGING YOUR
PERFECTS! REMEMBER IT CAN
BE ANYTHING –
DAYS, MOMENTS, FOOD,
EXPERIENCES, FEELINGS,
BOOKS, MUSIC........

THIS IS ABOUT YOU!

Go!

......remember to colour as you go!

Examples

10/1/15

Horrible day...
Bath, bubbles, book & chill tonight - perfect!

20/06/16

Unexpected early finish at work!
Thank you!

10/10/15

'R U OK?'
Text from a friend made my day.

20/02/16
Pizza ✓ check
Wine ✓ check
DVD ✓ check
Fire ✓ check
Duvet ✓ check
PERFECT!

STOP and take a moment in every day to appreciate something - whether it be a quiet cuppa, a cuddle with a loved one, a beautiful sound, a fabulous view, or something tiny that you can appreciate - and log it! You will be amazed at the journey you will log and enjoy.
Remember to smile!

My Perfects!
- week one -

date:

date:

date:

date:

date:

date:

date:

My Perfects!
- week two -

date:

date:

date:

date:

date:

date:

date:

Do something every day that makes you happy.

My Perfects!
- week three -

date:

date:

date:

date:

date:

date:

date:

My Perfects!
- week four -

date:

date:

date:

date:

date:

date:

date:

Random Acts of Kindness

I have put just 4 of these in each 4 week section but you can do more or less to suit you. This is about passing something 'perfect' onto someone else - I have put examples to give you an idea - they can be just TINY or even just a kind word or a 'Thank you' - it's surprising just how easily you can bring some sunshine or a smile into someone's life with a lovely small token act or words of kindness

Random Act

Date:

I gave a chocolate bar to a friend with a
card just to say 'Hello!'

Random Act

Date:

Bought a homeless person
a takeaway pizza

Random Act

Date:

Donated
a load of
clothes to my
local charity

Random Act

Date:

Told my bin men what a good job they do & a thank
you - goes a long way!

Random Act

Date:

My Random Acts of Kindness or Words

Random Act

Date:

Random Act

Date:

Random Act   Date:

TODAY IS FULL OF POSSIBILITIES -
YOU JUST HAVE TO BELIEVE!
I BELIEVE IN...

What do you believe in?
I believe in...

Collectables
(make a scrapbook of photos/receipts/leaflets week 1-4)

My Perfects!
- week five -

date:

date:

date:

date:

date:

date:

date:

My Perfects!
- week six -

date:

date:

date:

date:

date:

date:

date:

CHOOSE THE HAPPY PATH

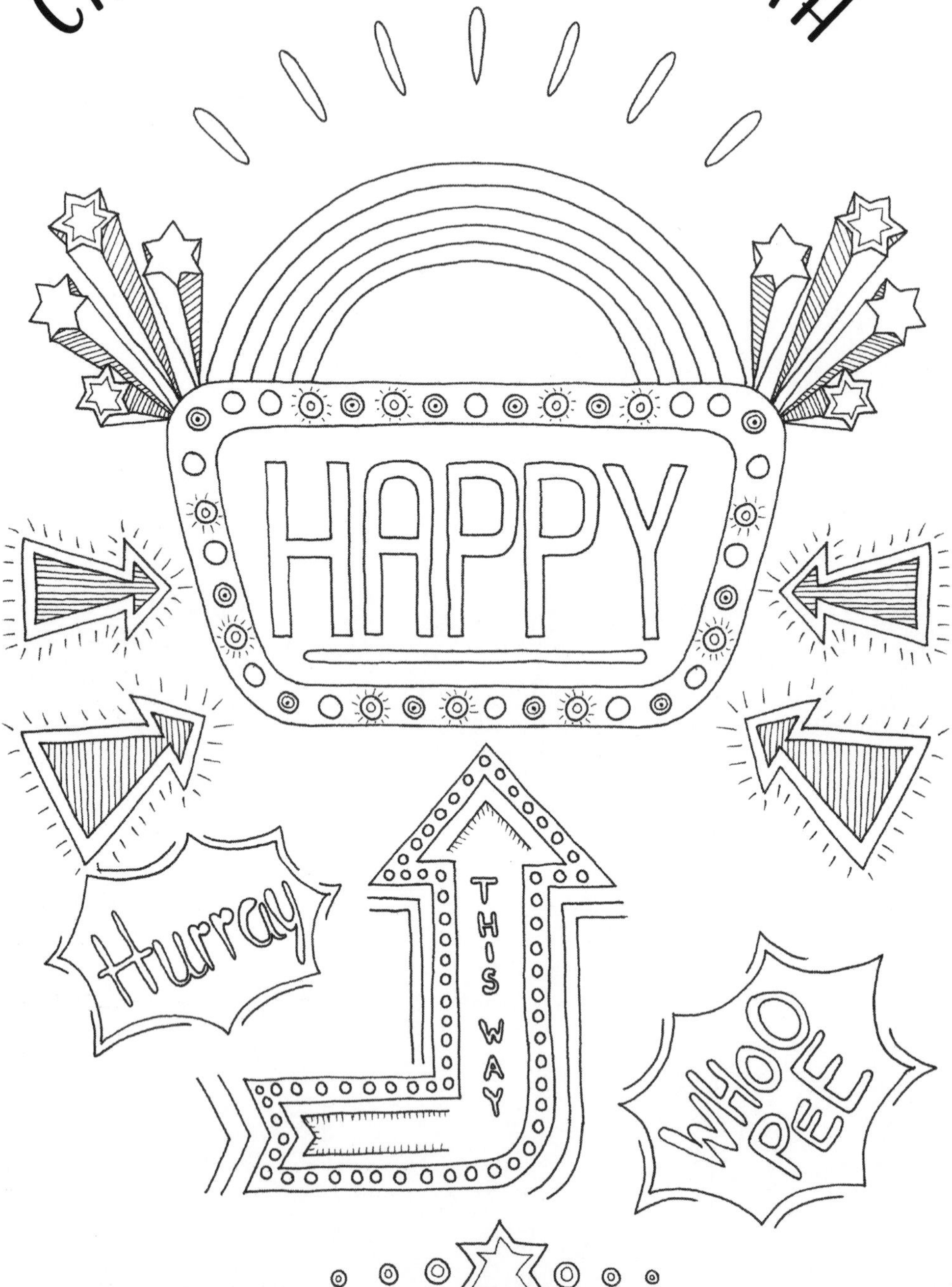

My Perfects!
- week seven -

date:

date:

date:

date:

date:

date:

date:

My Perfects!
- week eight -

date:

date:

date:

date:

date:

date:

date:

Random Act
Date:

My Random Acts of
Kindness or Words

Random Act
Date:

Random Act
Date:

Random Act   Date:

EVERYTHING IS POSSIBLE,
YOUR DREAMS,
YOUR IDEAS,
YOUR VISION...
NEVER LET ANYONE TELL YOU
YOU CAN'T.

I CAN!

A friend of mine wanted to learn to swim - she went for a lesson as a 36-year-old grown woman and the swimming instructor asked her 'so what can you do'....... 'well I can't swim for a start!'...... 'I asked you what CAN you do?!' - what CAN you do? This journal is logging all the good and positives about day-to-day living and life.

I CAN!

WHAT CAN **YOU** DO?

Collectables
(make a scrapbook of photos/receipts/leaflets week 5-8)

My Perfects!
- week nine -

date:

date:

date:

date:

date:

date:

date:

My Perfects!
- week ten -

date:

date:

date:

date:

date:

date:

date:

TODAY YOU ARE YOU,
THAT IS TRUER THAN
TRUE. THERE IS NO ONE
ALIVE. WHO IS YOUER THAN
THAN YOU!

(DR SUESS)

My Perfects!
- week eleven -

date:

date:

date:

date:

date:

date:

date:

date:

date:

date:

date:

date:

date:

date:

Random Act

Date:

My Random Acts of Kindness or Words

Random Act

Date:

Random Act

Date:

Random Act   Date:

WINDOW THEORY

OK, so here is my window theory — this is a true story and fundamentally changed how I live my life and how I now see other people's lives. It's a good reminder at times — it really is like looking through a window at someone's life. Often things aren't quite as they seem!

My view through the 'window'...

This is a true story, that I experienced many years ago.

I arrive at Sally's house for a training session that I am carrying out — I pull up on her drive in my little blue car which is not by any stretch of the imagination new! I park next to her two brand new BMWs outside her brand new 5-bedroomed house on the new estate on the smart side of town. Sally's good-looking husband opens the door, greets me and makes me a coffee while Sally is just finishing off getting ready upstairs. Sally breezes in looking amazing in designer jeans and a cotton top. Her husband hands her a coffee, gives her a kiss and goes out to work. We commence the day and start chatting (this is my first meeting with Sally). I am naturally a very chatty and nosy person and like to find out about people — Sally confirms she is nervous about the day as she is shy and not been out to work for a number of years and isn't good meeting new people. The house is full of photos of Sally and her three young children. It's an immaculate house with a big garden, trampoline and swing set. A perfect setting, a perfect family, a perfect life.

Or...a perfect lie?

I am seeing what Sally and her husband want me to see – the house, the clothes, the cars, the garden, the photos, the lifestyle – the reality is VERY different, sadly.

As the day progresses, Sally opens up to me and actually crumbles. She is lonely, unhappy and in a very bad place. She has no one to talk to, no friends locally and doesn't see her children – you see Sally was married for 15 years and has 3 children. She was very unhappy and had an affair with the window cleaner while her husband was out at work and her children were at school. One day her husband came home early...

She moved out in haste, taking a suitcase of clothes, as many photos as she could and she moved to the other side of town. She and the window cleaner moved in together, he lost a lot of work and is now going out daily to try and get new business. His car is a hire-purchase and so is Sally's and they are struggling to make the payments. They moved into the only house they could find at such short notice even though they don't need such a big place or such a high rent and she is now trying to get back into the workplace after many years at home. Her confidence was at an all-time low and she was living day-to-day in bleak unhappiness.

When I arrived, I was a bit in awe of Sally and what I saw to be her life – I have now learnt to take my time with people – sometimes it is EXACTLY as you see, but sometimes it can be very different! I had seen what I wanted to see from the outside – through the window – but the reality was far different. I have since been in touch with Sally. She now sees her children regularly, has met a new, lovely man who is a builder and they have got plans to build a house together and get married later this year – she works part time as a TA in a school and is very happy. This is not an isolated story – there are lots of people out there living a life that you only see through a window – just take a step back, look through some other windows, or step a little closer to look in – these people may not be all you think and may need a friend too. xx

EVERYTHING YOU WERE LOOKING FOR WAS RIGHT THERE WITH YOU ALL ALONG.

(THE WIZARD OF OZ)

Collectables

(make a scrapbook of photos/receipts/leaflets week 9-12)

My Perfects!
- week thirteen -

date:

date:

date:

date:

date:

date:

date:

My Perfects!
- week fourteen -

date:

date:

date:

date:

date:

date:

date:

YOU HAVE BRAINS IN YOUR HEAD.
YOU HAVE FEET IN YOUR SHOES.
YOU CAN STEER YOURSELF IN ANY DIRECTION YOU CHOOSE.
(DR SUESS)

My Perfects!
- week fifteen -

date:

date:

date:

date:

date:

date:

date:

date:

date:

date:

date:

date:

date:

date:

Random Act
Date:

My Random Acts of Kindness or Words

Random Act
Date:

Random Act
Date:

Random Act   Date:

'PERFECT'

My perfect and yours may be similar or polar opposites – it is things to me that I take from day-to-day life and enjoy and appreciate. No one is really perfect but your perception of them and their lives may lead you to believe they are. Social Media is brilliant – I do love it and it has its place – I have learnt though, that it can be very dangerous. People will only put out the best photos, the best updates and the perfect image of them and their families and lives – it can make you feel very isolated, left out and envious at times. This is a snapshot of their 'perfects' – their lives are most likely not always like this.

This journal is like a private catalogue of your life. It can be shown off if you wish, but this is your journey and your log and your life. Do you really want everyone to be privy to all your perfect moments? It's about what makes YOU happy and your closest people that matter – not everyone else. Live life for you and not to please and impress others. I expect you'll be far happier and less stressed. Take just a little time for you – enjoy more out of every day. Find a 'perfect' in each day.

Ten Perfects!

A simple but lovely way to start appreciating the little things around us that we take for granted. I do this list regularly and sometimes I make it generic – ten perfects about my life, the world in general and sometimes I make it more specific and do my ten perfects for the day! I also do this with my young children too – really refreshing to see what they put and how they see the perfect in such simple things! Since doing this excercise I have found so many more things in my life to be happy about and lots of imperfect perfects!

My ten generic perfects (Sept 2016)

- The sound of birds singing
- Having a flexible job that allows me to have time with my children
- The world for being so diverse and amazing
- The sky that changes with every moment
- The weather that makes us appreciate the sunshine days
- Having all my senses
- My family and my lovely freinds
- Music
- Living in the country
- Having a car and being able to drive!

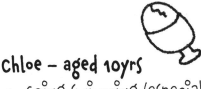

Chloe – aged 10yrs

- Going swimming (especially wave rave on a weds!)
- Laughing – it makes me feel happy
- Ice cream, any flavour
- The rain and the sun that helps the flowers to grow
- Flowers that feed the bees
- Books – I love reading
- My family and cuddles
- The snow so I can build a snowman
- My bed and sleeping!
- Singing, music and drama

DINOSAURS

Hayden – aged 8 yrs

- Lego
- Starwars
- Dinosaurs
- Swimming
- Rugby
- Sleeping
- Eggs – dunky are the best!
- Being tickled
- Milk – proper full fat pls
- Bugs

One of my daughter's ten one day was ' I am so happy that the world is spinning so I can't fall off'! I love this and found it really poignant – we can't fall off so we should embrace it and enjoy the spin!

MY 10 PERFECTS!

-
-
-
-
-
-
-
-
-
-

I LOVE doing this excercise with my kids — it makes me realise how simple things can be - so important and to enjoy the little things — their 'perfect' lists are refreshing and simple — PERFECT!

My Ten perfects today by chloe aged 10 (28/10/16)

- No school today!
- Playdate with my friend (BFF!)
- Watching clips of Mamma Mia on you tube
- Meeting a new friend
- Playing on the trampoline
- Doing well in my riding lesson — (I jumped!)
- Was allowed to stay up late as no school tomorrow — yeah!!!!
- Cuddles with my Mum
- Hot chocolate
- Riding my bike

My Ten perfects today by Hayden aged 8 (22/10/16)

- Jumping my pony — feels like flying!
- Ice cream!
- Playing on my skateboard
- Spending time with my family
- My bathtime tonight
- Having cuddles in bed this morning — no school!
- Seeing Lydia — I like her
- Playing on the trampoline
- Doing my lego
- Snuggling down in my bed

My Ten Perfects TODAY! 10/10/16

- I woke up before the alarm!
- My morning cuppa
- The sun is shining
- The smell of fresh cut grass
- The birds singing
- My latest fav song was on the radio
- Cuddles with my kids
- Hot bath tonight
- Good sales at work
- Doing some Christmas shopping online!

MY 10 PERFECTS!

-
-
-
-
-
-
-
-
-
-

TODAY

STOP WAITING FOR FRIDAY, FOR SUMMER, FOR SOMEONE TO FALL IN LOVE WITH YOU FOR LIFE. HAPPINESS IS ACHIEVED WHEN YOU STOP WAITING FOR IT AND MAKE THE MOST OF THE MOMENT YOU ARE IN NOW!

PERFECT ME!

10 THINGS OTHERS LOVE ABOUT ME (ASK FRIENDS AND FAMILY TO TELL YOU ONE OR TWO THINGS THEY LIKE ABOUT YOU)

1

2

3

4

5

6

7

8

9

10

Collectables
(make a scrapbook of photos/receipts/leaflets week 13-16)

My Perfects!
- week seventeen -

date:

date:

date:

date:

date:

date:

date:

My Perfects!
- week eighteen -

date:

date:

date:

date:

date:

date:

date:

THE MOST IMPORTANT THING IS TO
ENJOY YOUR LIFE - TO BE HAPPY IS
ALL THAT MATTERS.

My Perfects!
- week nineteen -

date:

date:

date:

date:

date:

date:

date:

My Perfects!
- week twenty -

date:

date:

date:

date:

date:

date:

date:

Random Act

Date:

My Random Acts of Kindness or Words

Random Act

Date:

Random Act

Date:

Random Act   Date:

Can't see the woods for the trees? Sometimes in life we can't find our way or our direction – we are so busy juggling and trudging on and get overwhelmed. This is when it's time to STOP, take stock and find a different path so we can move into the clearing and see not only the woods, but the glimmers of sunshine streaming through too.

A very good friend of mine helped me with this many years ago and I find it really helps – if you are feeling overwhelmed and need to take stock, this exercise may help you, it's worth a try and works for me!

Imagine you are an airplane – speeding down the runway, ready to take off. Every time you try and take off and lift the plane's nose, you keep failing. Each time you try, you end up going faster and faster but failing to take off with each attempt. This is when it's time to STOP! You need to stop your plane, disembark and take out all the luggage in the hold. It is weighing down the plane and stopping you from taking off.

Now, take all your bags out and arrange them in no particular order on the tarmac (the bags are all your troubles, worries, burdens, and the good things) – you need to decide which bags are going back on the plane and which need to be left on the tarmac. Get rid of the bag with the broken zip, the tatty carrier bag, the old rucksack (these could be bad relationships, bad friends, horrible job, excess clutter in the house that is stressing you – anything at all!) Once you have decided which bags to keep (the Gucci, the Prada, the quality in your life that makes you happy) then you need to work on taking the rubbish to the tip – don't get me wrong, this can take time and can be emotional. Remember to keep strong and look for the little perfects that will keep you focused – these bags are the rubbish and trash that are slowing you down, making you unhappy and stopping your plane from taking off. Once you have got rid of the trash, you will be able to load up your quality baggage and your plane will take off and fly! This exercise helped me through many a bad time – I still regularly stop my plane and access my luggage – maybe not as often as I should, but we're working on that one! Enjoy your plane journey.

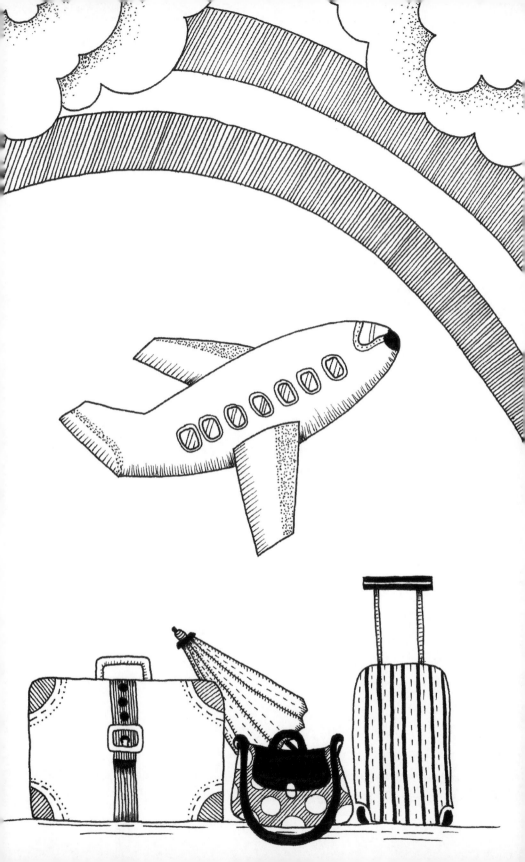

Collectables
(make a scrapbook of photos/receipts/leaflets week 17-20)

My Perfects!
- week twenty-one -

date:

date:

date:

date:

date:

date:

date:

My Perfects!
- week twenty-two -

date:

date:

date:

date:

date:

date:

date:

WHY FIT IN WHEN
YOU WERE BORN TO STAND
OUT.

DR SUESS

My Perfects!
- week twenty-three -

date:

date:

date:

date:

date:

date:

date:

My Perfects!
- week twenty-four -

date:

date:

date:

date:

date:

date:

date:

Random Act

Date:

My Random Acts of Kindness or Words

Random Act

Date:

Random Act

Date:

Random Act   Date:

Write yourself a letter -

tell yourself all about YOU, what you do, what are you like? Who are your friends, what are your favourite things to do, what makes you laugh, who are you? And don't forget to date it!

Once you've done a letter to yourself then write a letter (handwritten!) to 5 close friends, tell them what you like about them, what you remember about when you first met, what you think they are brilliant at, how they make you feel etc - anything at all but the challenge is to do a handwritten (no cheating!) letter and post it - it will make someone's day!

Attach your letter here!

Collectables
(make a scrapbook of photos/receipts/leaflets week 21-24)

date:

date:

date:

date:

date:

date:

date:

date:

date:

date:

date:

date:

date:

date:

LOOK FOR SOMETHING
PERFECT IN EACH DAY,
EVEN WHEN YOU HAVE
TO LOOK A LITTLE
HARDER. LET THE
CHALLENGES MAKE
YOU STRONGER.

date:

date:

date:

date:

date:

date:

date:

My Perfects!
- week twenty-eight -

date:

date:

date:

date:

date:

date:

date:

Random Act

Date:

My Random Acts of Kindness or Words

Random Act

Date:

Random Act

Date:

Random Act   Date:

TICKET TO
YOUR PERFECT
DESTINATION

Where would you love to travel to?

LIFE IS A JOURNEY - NOT A DESTINATION.

ENJOY THE JOURNEY.

My perfect day on holiday. Postcard to myself!

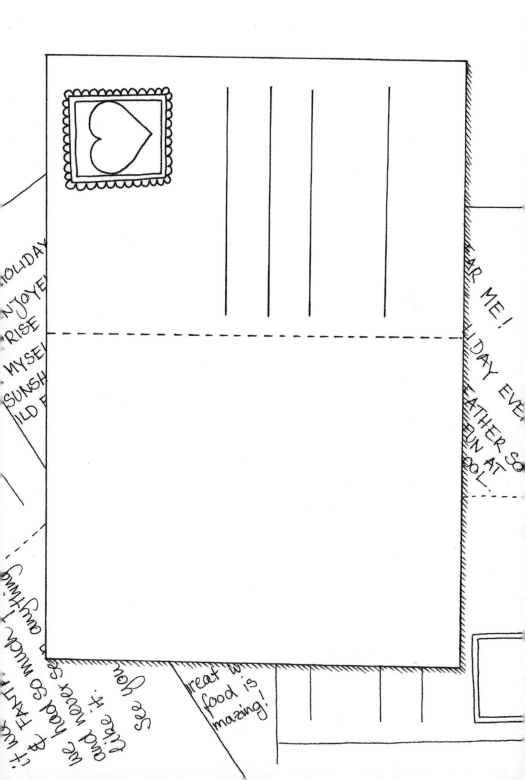

PERFECT TRIP? WHO WITH, WHERE DID YOU GO? PERFECT MOMENTS?

PERFECT HOLIDAY RETURN TICKET

NAMES:

DATE:

TIME:

DESTINATION:

Collectables
(make a scrapbook of photos/receipts/leaflets week 25-28)

My Perfects!
- week twenty-nine -

date:

date:

date:

date:

date:

date:

date:

My Perfects!
- week thirty-

date:

date:

date:

date:

date:

date:

date:

My Perfects!
- week thirty-one -

date:

date:

date:

date:

date:

date:

date:

My Perfects!
- week thirty-two -

date:

date:

date:

date:

date:

date:

date:

Random Act

Date:

My Random Acts of Kindness or Words

Random Act

Date:

Random Act

Date:

Random Act   Date:

TOXIC 'FRIENDS'

Now this is a toughie! We all (well, the majority of us) like to be liked. We will go out of our way with people and go above and beyond for our friends. Sometimes, unintentionally we attract toxic friends and relationships – this isn't to say the friend is bad or intentionally upsetting us (although this unfortunately CAN sometimes be the case), I just think that we have people that sometimes are not good or positive for us in our lives. Now, I'm not saying go out and ditch anyone that has been horrible to you or that drains you emotionally (although if someone is constantly putting you down and horrible, WHY would you want them to be your friend?!) What I am saying is try and reduce your liaisons with these people. Take a good long, hard look at your friends, your social circle and spend more time with the people and groups that make you feel good. I do get that this is easier said than done, but believe me it is a really good way to detox your head and get more perfects in your life.

I have some amazing friends, a fabulous family and enjoy some great times with them. I am just aware that I am quite a vulnerable personality at times and open to be hurt. I dwell on things generally and allow toxic people to come into my life and drain me mentally. Just take some time to think about this and if you can, try to reduce the toxic elements in your life. Also, be aware YOU may be toxic at times to others and by being more positive and seeing the little perfects, it can actually help others too!

Your Happy Place!

Go (either physically or mentally) to your 'happy place' – I have a number of places that I love and have happy memories or just make me feel happy to be there –

- The 'locals' beach in Croatia
- My Garden
- Just being on or around my horse
- Walking in the woods – not any specific woods, I just love trees at any time of the year!
- My BFF's house – drinking coffee or wine!
- My kitchen – usually on a Friday eve with family
- Cambodia – Just the most AMAZING holiday EVER!
- My bed
- In my car, driving with the music or radio on when I am not in a rush to get to my destination and I can just enjoy the journey
- Almost anywhere with my husband and children – they make me happy!
- My office (my little escape place!)

MY HAPPY PLACES LIST

*

*

*

*

*

*

*

*

*

*

WHAT MAKES ME FEEL HAPPY GENERALLY DAY-TO-DAY?

MY HAPPY LIST

*
*
*
*
*
*
*
*
*
*

What makes you happy? Do more of what makes you happy.....
Why not?!

Collectables
(make a scrapbook of photos/receipts/leaflets week 29-32)

date:

date:

date:

date:

date:

date:

date:

My Perfects!
- week thirty-four -

date:

date:

date:

date:

date:

date:

date:

date:

date:

date:

date:

date:

date:

date:

My Perfects!
- week thirty-six -

date:

date:

date:

date:

date:

date:

date:

PERFECT
WISHES

Fill the tree with
your VIP wishes

Colour me in

> One day Alice came to a fork in the road and saw a Cheshire Cat in a tree. 'Which road do I take?' she asked. 'Where do you want to go?' was his response. 'I don't know,' Alice answered. 'Then,' said the cat, 'it doesn't matter.'

(Alice in Wonderland)

WHERE HAVE YOU BEEN?

WHERE DO YOU WANT TO GO?

Collectables
(make a scrapbook of photos/receipts/leaflets week 33-36)

date:

date:

date:

date:

date:

date:

date:

My Perfects!
- week thirty-eight -

date:

date:

date:

date:

date:

date:

date:

BE WHO YOU ARE AND SAY
WHAT YOU FEEL BECAUSE
THOSE WHO MIND,
DON'T MATTER. AND THOSE
WHO MATTER, DON'T MIND!

DR SUESS

My Perfects!
- week thirty-nine -

date:

date:

date:

date:

date:

date:

date:

My Perfects!
- week forty -

date:

date:

date:

date:

date:

date:

date:

Random Act

Date:

My Random Acts of Kindness or Words

Random Act

Date:

Random Act

Date:

Random Act   Date:

Mindfulness of NOW!

A friend of mine introduced me to this and I love it and it has helped me enormously – I do this over a cup of tea daily and also if I ever get 5 minutes downtime in the day (very rare but usually when I am sitting in the car waiting for school pick up or waiting in a swimming lesson or similar!) The mindfulness of NOW is so strong and can help so much for the 'fretters' or worriers of us (I include myself in this category!) If you had a bad day yesterday, had a falling out or a bad experience, it is way too easy to dwell on this and play it over and over in your mind. You can replay the situation or conversation AS MUCH as you like or want but you physically cannot change what has happened and been and gone. You can then spend a lot of mental time, energy and stressing playing out in your mind how you could have behaved, what you should have said and what the different outcome would be...or you can start deciding how you are going to address this issue next time, what you are going to do, say what will happen, etc. You can then stress a bit more, worry a bit harder and still not change the before, the after or the maybe of the situation. You can't change yesterday and you can't write tomorrow so enjoy the NOW! Take 5 minutes and just enjoy the NOW – and jot down all the good stuff that is happening now.

Collectables

(make a scrapbook of photos/receipts/leaflets week 37-40)

My Perfects!
- week forty-one -

date:

date:

date:

date:

date:

date:

date:

My Perfects!
- week forty-two -

date:

date:

date:

date:

date:

date:

date:

THE WORD 'IMPERFECT' ACTUALLY SPELLS ' I'M PERFECT ' BECAUSE EVERYONE IS PERFECT IN THEIR OWN IMPERFECT WAYS!

My Perfects!
- week forty-three -

date:

date:

date:

date:

date:

date:

date:

My Perfects!
- week forty-four -

date:

date:

date:

date:

date:

date:

date:

BUCKET LIST

They say 'Life is short' (WHO are they anyway?!) but whatever!
Life is short – most of us don't have any idea of how long or short our
lives will be, some people get poorly and then do a bucket list of things
to do and some don't have a chance – WHY wait to do a bucket list?
Do it now while you can and while you can enjoy it fully and appreciate
it – it doesn't have to be a wild list or expensive if you don't want – or
it can have some completely random, wild, wacky expensive stuff!

I started my bucket list many years ago and add on to it regulary and
cross things off – sometimes not so regularly but I do review it and I'm
constantly updating it!
What's your bucket list?

My bucket list - 1/1/16

1. Wild swimming - done; bloody cold but ace!

2. White water rafting -

3. fun ride with Hayden -

4. Ride on the beach - done in Cambodia on hols

5. Earn enough money to not worry - (hmmm)

6. Finish my book - if you're reading this then done!

7. Run/get fit!

8. Travel - a whole list of countries! need a separate list for this!

9. Combat my fear of skiing

10. Do more (proper) photography

MY
BUCKET
LIST

Random Act

Date:

My Random Acts of
Kindness or Words

Random Act

Date:

Random Act

Date:

Random Act   Date:

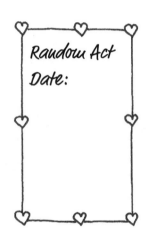

SOMETIMES I HALE BELIEVED IN AS MANY AS 6 IMPOSSIBLE THINGS BEFORE BREAKFAST.

(alice in wonderland)

.... AND WHY NOT

Collectables

(make a scrapbook of photos/receipts/leaflets week 41-44)

date:

date:

date:

date:

date:

date:

date:

My Perfects!
- week forty-six -

date:

date:

date:

date:

date:

date:

date:

I JUST WANT
TO LIVE MY LIFE.
WHILE I'M ALIVE.
IT'S MY LIFE.
BON JOVI.

My Perfects!
- week forty-seven -

date:

date:

date:

date:

date:

date:

date:

My Perfects!
- week forty-eight -

date:

date:

date:

date:

date:

date:

date:

Random Act

Date:

My Random Acts of Kindness or Words

Random Act

Date:

Random Act

Date:

Random Act   Date:

Anger is a pill that you swallow hoping to make someone else ill. You can lie there at 3.30 am feeling rage and anger at someone or something and yet they have NO IDEA you are doing this – we are the ones feeling the upset, hurt and rage – NOT them! Think about any time you have felt like this and all the harm you are doing is to yourself and no one else –

PLEASE don't swallow the anger pill – you owe it to yourself to let it go however you can – I actually use songs either in my car, at home or in my head! My anger pill song is literally (sadly!) the song from Disney's Frozen – Let it Go! This works a treat for me but I have a whole list of anger pill songs.

* DON'T WORRY ABOUT THE FUTURE; OR WORRY, *
  BUT KNOW THAT WORRYING IS AS EFFECTIVE AS
* TRYING TO SOLVE AN ALGEBRA EQUATION BY *
* CHEWING BUBBLEGUM. *

  BAZ LUHRMANN-

MY 'PERFECT' PLAYLIST - A FEW LYRICS!

(MY LIST IS MUCH LONGER BUT I HAVE JUST PUT
10 TO GIVE YOU A TASTER!)

TAYLOR SWIFT - SHAKE IT OFF
FROZEN - LET IT GO
THE LIGHT HOUSE FAMILY - HIGH
LOU REED - PERFECT DAY
JAMES MORRISON - ONE LIFE
BAZ LUHRMANN - WEAR SUNSCREEN
AMERICAN-AUTHORS - BEST DAY OF MY LIFE
ONE REPUBLIC - SOMETHING I NEED
BEYONCE - I WAS HERE
PHARRELL WILLIAMS - HAPPY

'IF I KNEW YESTERDAY WHAT I KNOW TODAY,
WHERE WOULD I BE TOMORROW? I WON'T LET
MY SOUL SLIDE AWAY, I'D DO WHATEVER IT
TAKES COS THIS TIME IS BORROWED. I GOT ONE
LIFE. ONE LIFE, ONE LIFE AND I AM GONNA
LIVE IT, I GOT ONE LIFE, ONE LIFE, ONE LIFE
AND I'M GONNA LIVE IT RIGHT...'
JAMES MORRISON.

my perfect playlist

What's your anger pill song list? Try it.... it works and makes for a happier time - remember you are only hurting yourself if you don't let it go (this is tough I know but it can help) x

I'M NEVER GONNA LOOK BACK
WHOA, I'M NEVER GONNA GIVE IT UP
NO, PLEASE DON'T WAKE ME NOW

THIS IS GONNA BE THE BEST DAY OF MY LIFE
MY LI-I-I-I-IFE

THIS IS GONNA BE THE BEST DAY OF MY LIFE
MY LI-I-I-IFE

AMERICAN AUTHORS

I WAS HERE
I LIVED, I LOVED
I WAS HERE
I DID, I'VE DONE, EVERYTHING THAT I WANTED
AND IT WAS MORE THAN I THOUGHT IT WOULD BE
I WILL LEAVE MY MARK SO EVERYONE WILL KNOW
I WAS HERE

BEYONCÉ

'LIKE A SMALL BOAT. ON THE OCEAN. SENDING
BIG WAVES, INTO MOTION. LIKE HOW A SINGLE
WORD, CAN MAKE A HEART OPEN. I MIGHT ONLY
HAVE ONE MATCH, BUT I CAN MAKE AN EXPLOSION.
AND ALL THOSE THINGS I DIDN'T SAY. WRECKING
BALLS INSIDE MY BRAIN. I WILL SCREAM THEM
LOUD TONIGHT. CAN YOU HEAR MY VOICE THIS TIME?

THIS IS MY FIGHT SONG. TAKE BACK
MY LIFE SONG, PROVE I'M ALRIGHT
SONG.' RACHEL PLATTEN

Choose your very own song lyrics and fill this wonderful space right up with them. The possibilities are endless, so have fun and get writing

Collectables

(make a scrapbook of photos/receipts/leaflets week 45-48)

My Perfects!
- week forty-nine -

date:

date:

date:

date:

date:

date:

date:

My Perfects!
- week fifty -

date:

date:

date:

date:

date:

date:

date:

IT'S NOT WHERE YOU GO, IT'S WHO YOU MEET ON THE WAY.

WIZARD OF OZ

My Perfects!
- week fifty-one -

date:

date:

date:

date:

date:

date:

date:

My Perfects!
- week fifty-two -

date:

date:

date:

date:

date:

date:

date:

Collectables
(make a scrapbook of photos/receipts/leaflets week 49-52)

So, we come to the end of our journey for now – I hope you have enjoyed logging your 'perfects' and you are enjoying big or little moments that bring you happiness and some joy. This journal is a keepsake to remind you of just how perfect things really are if you just can take a moment to enjoy them. The more you enjoy your perfect moments, occasions and times, the more you will find them without looking.

I hope this journal will give you a suitcase full of memories and lots of lovely 'perfects' to look back on and remember.

Wishing you all the best,
AJ xx

Acknowledgements

Gratitude in abundance for all the lovely people who have supported me on this journey and believed in the concept!

Firstly PMG, excuse the cliché but my bff, my rock, my support and the one who believes in me always, even when I doubt myself (which is often) and the one who is there for me through all my madcap ideas and adventures -
THANK YOU - ily x

Sue Miller (and TeamAuthorUK!) my amazing friend who held my hand from the beginning, Ellen Parzer who put her artistic talents to work magically, Frankie who penned my quotes, to all the gorgeous people I have met on the way and Moomin who booted me up the bum to make me do this.

And, not forgetting all my long-suffering friends and family who have endured my tears, tantrums, highs and lows (you all know who you are!) – thank you x

To follow AJ Gill and find out more about the 'hidden perfects' in life:

F: @hiddenperfects
T: @hiddenperfects
Instagram: hiddenperfects

Printed in Great Britain
by Amazon